[ P O E T R Y ]

*The Location of Things* [1960]

*Poems: The Location of Things,
Archaics, The Open Skies* [1962]

*Robert Goodnough, Painter* [1962]

*The Blue Stairs* [1968]

*The I Ching* [1969]

*Moscow Mansions* [1973]

*The Countess from Minneapolis*
[1976, 1991]

*The Türler Losses* [1979]

*Biography* [1980]

*Quilts* [1981]

*Nudes* [1986]

*Musicality* [1988]

*Fair Realism* [1989, 1996]

*The Altos* [1992]

*Defensive Rapture* [1992]

*Selected Poems* [1995]

*Stripped Tales* [1995]

*Quill, Solitary Apparition* [1996]

*The Luminous* [1999]

*Strings* [1999]

*Outside of This, That Is* [1999]

*Rocks on a Platter* [1999]

*If So, Tell Me* [1999]

*The Confetti Trees: Motion
Picture Stories* [1999]

*Symbiosis* [2000]

*Miniatures and Other Poems* [2002]

[ F I C T I O N ]

*Seeking Air* [1978, 1997]

[ N O N - F I C T I O N ]

*Herself Defined: The Poet H.D.
and Her World* [1985, 2002]

*Durer in the Window:
Reflexions on Art* [2003]

*Forces of Imagination:
Writing on Writing* [2003]

[ P L A Y S ]

*The Ladies Choice* [1953]

*The Office: A One Act Play
in Three Scenes* [1960]

*Port: A Murder in One Act* [1964]

*The Diving Board* [1966]

*Chinese Ghost Restaurant* [1967]

*The Swimming Pool* [1975]

*Often* [2000]

# The Red Gaze

WESLEYAN POETRY    WESLEYAN UNIVERSITY PRESS

# The Red Gaze

# Gaze

# Barbara Guest

MIDDLETOWN, CONNECTICUT

PUBLISHED BY WESLEYAN UNIVERSITY PRESS

MIDDLETOWN, CT 06459

WWW.WESLEYAN.EDU/WESPRESS

© 2005 BY BARBARA GUEST

DESIGN AND COMPOSITION BY QUEMADURA

PRINTED IN THE UNITED STATES OF AMERICA

5    4    3    2    1

LIBRARY OF CONGRESS CATALOGING-IN-PUBLICATION DATA

GUEST, BARBARA.

THE RED GAZE / BARBARA GUEST.

P.  CM. — (WESLEYAN POETRY)

ISBN 0-8195-6750-7 (CLOTH : ALK. PAPER)

I. TITLE. II. SERIES.

PS3513.U44R43 2004

811'.54 — DC22

2004021221

# Contents

1

2

1

# Nostalgia

Hands are touching.
You began in cement in small spaces.
You began the departure. Leaves restrain. You attempted the departure.
A smile in sunshine, nostalgia.
Beneath shadow of shadows of Columbus the Navigator. Waving farewell.
Street, shadows.


I have lost my detachment, sparrow with silver teeth.
I have lost the doves of Milan, floating politely.


        Recognize me, I shall be here, O Nietzsche.
        We have skipped down three pairs of stairs,
they are not numbered, they are oddly assorted, velvet.


        Recognize me in sunshine.
Bulletins permit us to be freer than in Rome.
Castles perched on a cliff.
Filled with pears and magic.

I am not detached,

bulletins permit us comb, fish of silver.
A part of the tower
beckons to us.

# An Afternoon
# in Jeopardy

Piece of tapestry with bird sewed on.
A ruin from Rome, and in the background a rope.


Old Europe declares itself.


In the banquet hall birds nest.
A stranger causes the water to flow,
the alphabet is full of sorrow.


In the passageway sits the stranger.


He is without sin or sorrow or soldiers who mount their horses
and race up and down the farthingale hills.

He will not dine with the others.
They knew not he was an emperor
described as a poor man in disguise.


He has cast away his steel to rest beside the maiden.


Shadows are everywhere.          Oddness begins.

# Imagined Room

Do not forget the sky has other zones.

Let it rest on the embankment, close the eyes,

Lay it in the little bed made of maplewood.
Wash its sleeve in sky drops.

Let there be no formal potions.
A subject and a predicate made of glass.

You have entered the narrow zone
your portrait etched in glass.

Becoming less and less until the future faces you
like the magpie you hid,
exchanging feathers for other feathers.

In the tower you flew without wings
speaking in other tongues to the imagined room.

# Loneliness

Wounded,
the tower and green of the meadow below.


O meadow, O furnaces, royalty passes you.
Quick steps make a noise.


She rides on her palfrey, the maiden.
Bouquets fall from her green hair.


Shadows on grass reflect a loneliness everywhere.

O furnaces royalty passes you, quick steps make a noise.
She rides on her palfrey the maiden,
her green hair glistens.
How solitary!
Lo, on the river a monument passes by.

# A Different Honey

Close up shop

is what happens in Milan

and places older.

Who is protecting us,

we who were noticed by the Emperor

cruising in his vessel?

Remember navigators

tasting lemons from the trees

of their birthplace.

Do we know how they felt,

born under different signs?

Silent are honies in velvet cups.

# A Short Narrative

Your painting took a long time to dry.

It was sent to Rome to give it a royal luster.


Your thoughts the evening before had been gloomy.

They would not forget rumors accompanying you.


Lo, Royalty had placed a hand on your head.


Nobles twist their rings in corridors,

worried about painting's future.

# Freedom

Those at the excavation who followed the Dog Star
when he wandered, summit-catcher.
The days are unknown, the night also,
ending its speech. Sleeper on the grass,
dreamer of numbers.
Day, night, horoscope.

In the dark
we recognize
the shoreline is Vienna green.

Officials at Rome have ended the martyrdom.

# Alteration

In the sky a dilemma. Fountains rush by.
Home from the tournament beasts seek quiet.

Writing covers the desk.

               Your colonization of the infinite

               is a romantic departure.

I ask you to permit the image

             and the alteration of time.

# A Burst of Leaves

A burst of leaves announces your presence

                                           dropped from the frozen cloud.

Perhaps you are hiding, perhaps you have decided not to reveal

your singular presence.

                  The world conceals your identity from me.

                                  You once said we must abandon all risk.

You glanced at the idol

                within its burst of leaves.

A disappointed generation, words collapse around us.

Like the one who jumped into the sea. But the seas disappoint us, also.

We do not like to walk on their beaches, lined with laboratories and formula.

We are ready for a new orientation.

# The Next Floor

Hours become young days,
morning wrapped in reality.
Its heel turns a corner where the game
is played. Sensitive to the murmur outdoors,
I fold you in a warm fleece—
here is its cover, it will hide you until daybreak.


Smithies, ironworks, lattices to the next floor,
we are climbing. The urge enters to see more.
Destiny peers upward into a next stanza,
resting in the nearest hayrick,
adding up, taking away.
Of what use are stanzas in the dark,
ragamuffin?

# Roman Stripes

[ FOR JOHANNES BEILHARZ ]

What is new in the fostering world beyond.
We ask its name, created by indentation,
learned to avoid the shark's fin,
emerged from a world of fins.

Once it was thought the spiral staircase led us
to uncounted rings.
Tonight there is no other fin.
Tonight there is sorrow created by rings
tipped with green.

I saw the stair mount upward and could not stop
its climb until the heavens opened blinking,
until we felt suspension.
An odyssey parades in stripes.

# The Trickster

There is no system, no one writes in Greek.
It is empty here after the seismology,
one relies on sensibility that monitors
movement on a mountain top.

Corrective light that carried shadow away
to another visibility.

*Coyote before he opens his mouth.*
*Hidden in the canyon on a ledge*
*full of games and myth.*

# The Hungry Knight

Palest shadow on the middle rock,

Hungry knight! drifting.

O causes,

O celebrants,

massive,

comfort had ceased.


Massive night falls on the middle rock,

weighing-in like a scholar.

Heavy is the literature

bred on the rock,

filled with epiphany

night has known since infancy.

# The Past

The form of the poem subsided, it enters another poem.

A witness was found for the markings inscribed upside-down.

It might have been a celebration, so strong the presence

of the poem. The sky sinks slowly inside the past.

# Modernism

The dreamer enters the room wearing a garment of red cloth.

On his feet are shoes of magic, they will carry him hither and yon.

He has dipped his pen into magic ink and cleared

the ordinary from the room.


We too, have heard the midnight chime and reached for our silver spoon,

as midnight stirs a coffee cup we praise modernism.

Restless leaf modifies his poem.

# Green Numbers

Others are accustomed to this hat on the furnace step,

a mild disassociation from the garment shop.

A new pair of shoes you are welcome to,

and a brimmed hat to wear in the rain.

We are accustomed to a guarantee of rain, guarantee of thunder,

the take-off that leads to thunder on the holiday night.


Green numbers, a patois we are learning to speak.

Butterflies in the house you told us about.

# Stair of Our Youth

O reward us who fought in the brush,
in the deep stiletto branches grown low to the grass,
who have wandered with messages to other kingdoms,
and slept in their heavy beds.
We serve these masters and smile at their clumsiness,
as they slip on the stair. We are witness to the burned pages
of their books, to their Oriental games.
Riding over stones of borrowed pleasure
lends grace to the smooth mount of our youth.

# A Noise of Return

We have seen the bowl toppled by morning crickets,

or imagined so, on our imaginary route,

it leads through the mountain.

We are walking on a shadowy line gentle in its way.


Imagination has removed the harshness.

This is a filibuster of routes,

concealed is the icy stone you tripped on.

It turns rocks into stone and promises

to listen to the morning tympanum.

felicitudes!

creating another tympanum.

# Freed Color

The branches are placed in a wet cloth,
clover reaches out.


They cannot locate a blue vine.
Purple fills the agenda. Red is on the plant,
the setting of a hibiscus tree.
They are warned not to linger in the purple shade.


Are these bitter colors? Are they accompanied
by rhyme to cheer them when they cross
into that land where color is rare?


They hasten to make use of freed color
who bends to no one,
who dwells in a tent like rhythm
continuously rolled.

To stop the riot of color, to hasten the quiet paucity of rhythm,
to sleep when it is time.


And doors open into a narrow surprise.
The jingle of crystal follows you everywhere,
even into the whistling corridor.

# The Gold Tap

The arrival of a winter morning unclasping its bandeau of sleep.

Marionettes are late risers. They awake in late morning,

bringing their hands to the gold tap and drinking its rare waters.

# Minimal Sound

What we are becomes a memory, the hand may open a secret lock.

The poem enters on tiptoe, climbs the terrain,

weary, it listens to minimal sound, the slowed

tree branches are drawn on purpose, part of the same program.

# The Brown Vest

A robin's nest being towed on the sidewalk.

Somewhere a complement to his brown vest.

He is more lively than before.

In the future we must take him away from the sidewalk

and lend him the joy he expects.

Use earth colors, they build strong nests.

He combs his throat then locks the chapel

Of the Goddess in his home.

2

# The Red Gaze

Red, purple, brown Guardian leaf.

Complications of red enter the leaf

and it is more accomplished,

turning brown then gray in varying attitudes

after the snow begins. Colorful complications

disturb serenity, causing our eye

to wander over the shaking tree.


Morning began with a concert of white.

Blue enters later.

# A Dawn Walk

Who took the tapestry from off the wall?

Who removed the silver lining?

A dawn walk in the tousled hall.


Dissolve the curiosities,

Pierrot of the mountain.

In the Alps of your being there is trust.

Search for trust.

It may be in the Alps of your soul,

young squire who tends the furnace,

who remarks on landscape finery.

# No Longer Strangers

No longer strangers

in these zones of departure

somehow integrated in a

fashion to parade

and to laugh

and to write

of the old speech

in the looking glass room.

Distribute these newly sought wings of artifice,

for each raid on the moon,

we were told at the meeting of strangers

who were learning the new tongue.

Put these two meetings together!

you will notice it is all one speech,

and jocular.

# Hans Hofmann

She remembers

a rocky landscape.

bridges over the gorge

Heaviness in the white.

A sudden burst of color.

"Structure and sensation."

*Going each day to the park bench, she begins to absorb*

*her surroundings.*


*Each day the park grows colder.*

*Who is sitting at the end of the park bench?*


*He is the painter Hans Hofmann, he is a famous painter.*

*(this is true). Talking in an atmosphere of color.*


*Listening in an atmosphere of color.*

To invoke the unseen, to unmask it. Reality in a glass
of water. The mirror reveals heartstrings of reality.

Students preparing for the class and its famous master.

A deep red gaze through maple leaves.

Maple red now splashes the mountain.

The students need mirrors to orchestrate color.

Their master uses thick color.

"Even black is a color."

A cool purple begins to descend through increasing twilight.

The class begins to speak of cold. The class shivers and they laugh.

A pinch of red remains on Hofmann's palette knife.

It reminds him of the red of maple leaves.

# Vignettes

(Hofmann classes on chill afternoons).

(Independent thinking and foreign thought).

(Hofmann explains *Narrative*).

*Hofmann surrenders his brush.*

Return of the white chandelier.

# Echoes

Once more riding down to Venice on borrowed horses,

    the air free of misdemeanor, at rest in the inns of our fathers.

    Once again whiteness like the white chandelier.

    Echoes of other poems . . .

# Instructions

Mood and Form. Other pieces of literature.

Emphasis on content.

Distance lingers in her hand.

Figure moves backward from the door.

. . . Figure modified by light.

Remove figure from window.

# Composition

Lo, from the outside a poem is with us, of another composition.

Travelled from an antique place.

Writing, narrow and sparse, pungent as the lemon tree.

Difficult, spelling and montage.


We have built no large hall to labor in.

We sleep on small cushions for as long as we wish.


Our lives are composed with magic and euphony.

# Supposition

You are willing

to pass through the center

composed of independent poetics.

To rearrange rhyme,

while you gather its energy.

*In each genuine art work something appears that did not exist before.*

[ THEODOR ADORNO ]

Barbara Guest began writing in the 1950s as a member of the New York School of Poets, which also included John Ashbery, Frank O'Hara and James Schuyler. Her work is saturated in the visual arts and plays the abstract qualities of language against its sensuousness and materiality. She has published twenty-three volumes of poetry and five volumes of prose. Recent titles include *Dürer in the Window: Reflexions on Art* (2003), *Rocks on a Platter* (Wesleyan, 1999), a novel entitled *Seeking Air* (1996), and a biography, *Herself Defined: The Poet H.D. and Her World* (1984). Guest has earned many awards, including the Robert Frost Medal for Distinguished Lifetime Achievement from the Poetry Society of America, the Longwood Award, and the Lawrence Lipton Award for Literature.

Her previous book from Wesleyan University Press, *Miniatures and Other Poems* (2002), was selected by *Library Journal* as one of the Best Poetry Books of 2002.